Original title:
Between Worlds

Copyright © 2024 Creative Arts Management OÜ
All rights reserved.

Author: Lorenzo Barrett
ISBN HARDBACK: 978-9916-88-876-6
ISBN PAPERBACK: 978-9916-88-877-3

Interwoven Dreams and Shadows

In whispers soft the night unfolds,
A tapestry where time is told.
The stars like secrets gently gleam,
In every heart, a hidden dream.

Through branches bare, the moonlight weaves,
A shroud of dreams beneath the leaves.
Each shadow dances, sways in grace,
A fleeting wisp, a tender trace.

The dawn brings forth a golden hue,
As colors merge, a world anew.
Yet in our minds, the night prevails,
In every thought, a dream prevails.

We walk the line 'twixt dark and light,
As dreams take flight, in endless night.
Interwoven, our lives flow,
In shadows deep, our hopes will grow.

The Suspended Moment

In a breath held tight, we dwell,
Time drips slowly, casting its spell.
Eyes locked in silence, hearts align,
In this stillness, the world feels divine.

Dreams flicker like stars in the night,
Each thought a spark, a fleeting light.
Memory dances, soft on the breeze,
Suspended in moments, such sweet reprieve.

Lingering at the Edge

Standing on cliffs where shadows play,
The sun whispers secrets of the day.
Waves crash wildly, a haunting song,
Drawing us close, where we feel we belong.

A step back, and the world expands,
The edge holds wonder, with trembling hands.
Though fear flickers in the depths of the heart,
We linger here, at the edge, not apart.

Caresses of the Unfelt

In the quiet moments of twilight's sway,
Gentle breezes weave dreams that play.
Invisible touches, whispers so light,
They brush against skin, taking flight.

A sigh escapes in the fading glow,
Caresses unseen, where feelings flow.
In the depths of silence, we clearly find,
The language of the heart, unconfined.

Journeys of the Whispering Wind

Through ancient trees, the whispers glide,
A journey unfolds, nature's guide.
Carried across mountains, valleys so wide,
The wind knows secrets, where dreams reside.

It dances with leaves, a playful tease,
Tales of longing, carried with ease.
Each gust a story, woven in time,
The wind is a poet, with rhythm and rhyme.

The Twilight's Embrace

The sun dips low, a gentle sigh,
As shadows stretch across the sky.
Whispers of night begin to play,
In twilight's glow, the world turns gray.

Stars awaken, one by one,
The day is lost, the night begun.
A hush falls deep, the colors fade,
In twilight's grasp, all moments made.

Secrets in the Half-Light

In corners dark, where secrets lie,
Half-lit whispers pass us by.
The moon's soft light, a guiding hand,
Reveals the paths we seldom planned.

Footsteps echo on cobblestone,
Silent tales long since overgrown.
In the half-light, truths unfold,
Stories linger, brave and bold.

The Bridge of Subtle Currents

A bridge of dreams spans the divide,
Where hearts connect, and fears subside.
The currents flow, both strong and slow,
In whispered tones, the river's glow.

Below, the depth hides tales untold,
Of ancient voices, brave and bold.
Each step we take, a pulse, a beat,
On this bridge where waters meet.

Fleeting Moments of Elsewhere

A glance can spark a world anew,
Fleeting moments, slipping through.
In laughter shared, in silence found,
We trace our dreams on borrowed ground.

The past and future intertwine,
In this brief dance, your hand in mine.
Time escapes, we chase the light,
Fleeting moments, pure delight.

Where Realities Converge

In twilight's grasp, paths intertwine,
Whispers of worlds in shadows align.
A dance of fate, where dreams collide,
We find the truth that worlds must hide.

Fleeting moments twist and weave,
A tapestry of what we believe.
In silent spaces, echoes chime,
Unraveling threads of endless time.

Hearts beat soft, in sync, they move,
Caught in the rhythm, they must prove.
Each choice a step, each glance a sign,
Where all our destinies intertwine.

In this embrace, we rise, we fall,
In the silence, we hear the call.
As colors blend and shadows merge,
We stand together, where worlds converge.

The Interlude of Existence

Life's fleeting pause, a breath in time,
Moments hang still, a whispered rhyme.
Between the tick and tock we find,
The essence of what binds mankind.

In echoes soft, the stories play,
Fragments of light in the shades of gray.
Time dances lightly on the edge,
Leaving us questions like an unmade pledge.

Hold tight the silence, embrace the hush,
In this in-between, feel the rush.
A flicker of stars in vast unknown,
In the interlude, our souls have grown.

Each heartbeat sings, a tale unspooled,
In the quiet space, we are all ruled.
Existence sways, a gentle tide,
In this calm, we learn to abide.

Cracks in the Fabric of Reality

Through the seams of time, light creeps in,
A shimmer of hope where shadows begin.
In the fractures, we seek the whole,
Finding connection deep in the soul.

Woven moments, fragile yet strong,
In the tapestry, we find where we belong.
Each thread a story, a hidden scar,
We stitch together, no matter how far.

The fabric trembles, whispers of fate,
In the silence, the echoes await.
Beyond the cracks, the universe sings,
Revealing the power of unseen things.

With every break, a chance to mend,
In the chaos, we learn to blend.
For in the gaps, the truths appear,
In the broken, we uncover the near.

Glimpses Beyond the Veil

Layers of mist obscure the night,
Behind the veil, there shines a light.
With every shiver, secrets unfold,
Whispered dreams of the brave and bold.

In twilight's haze, we dare to see,
Boundless realms of what could be.
Glimmers of truth in the shadows play,
Teasing our hearts to find the way.

A flutter of wings, a brush of grace,
Within the stillness, we find our place.
Messages carried on the cool breeze,
Revealing wonders that put us at ease.

As we peer through the curtain of time,
Each glimpse a note in existence's rhyme.
Together we'll tread, hand in hand,
Into the magic of the promised land.

Tangled in the Space Between

In the twilight, secrets hide,
Whispers linger, hearts collide.
Stars like threads in velvet skies,
Dreams take flight, unbound by ties.

Every glance, a silent plea,
Echoes of what used to be.
Time, a river flowing slow,
Winds of change begin to blow.

Between the breath, a silent song,
Notes of heartstrings, soft and strong.
In the shadows, hope resides,
Tangled paths where love abides.

The Silent Meeting of Horizons

Where the sky meets the endless sea,
Colors blend in harmony.
Sunsets cast a golden hue,
Silent meetings, me and you.

Gentle waves caress the shore,
Whispers of dreams we can't ignore.
In the distance, a promise glows,
As the twilight slowly flows.

Moments suspended, time stands still,
In the silence, we feel the thrill.
Horizons stretch, a vast expanse,
In this stillness, we take a chance.

Ghosts of the In-Between

Flickering lights in shadowed halls,
Whispers echo, memory calls.
Figures dance in twilight's embrace,
Fleeting glimpses of a face.

Between the worlds, they softly glide,
Veils of time where dreams abide.
Lost in thoughts of what once was,
Haunting whispers bring a pause.

In the spaces, where silence grows,
Ghostly secrets, no one knows.
Yet in their dance, we find our peace,
In the in-between, our fears release.

The Path Woven with Shadows

Underneath the ancient trees,
The path winds softly with the breeze.
Each step taken whispers low,
Stories hidden in the flow.

Shadows dance like fleeting thoughts,
Carried by the ties we've fought.
Through the dark, we find the light,
Woven dreams that take to flight.

In the rustle, a secret shared,
Steps of hope, though hearts have bared.
A journey forged in twilight's glow,
Together on this path we know.

Waking into the Unfamiliar

Morning light spills softly,
Chasing shadows from my room.
Familiar corners whisper,
Yet the air feels like a tomb.

Steps tread on paths uncharted,
Each sigh a gentle breeze.
Eyes wide, they search the silence,
For secrets, hidden keys.

Birds sing a new beginning,
Notes twirling in the sky.
A dance of dreams unfolding,
As moments drift and fly.

The world hums with fresh colors,
Painting life anew each day.
In this realm of bright uncertainty,
I find my endless way.

Lost in the Interstice

Between the click of seconds,
Time sways like a velvet strand.
Caught in a fleeting whisper,
I reach with a trembling hand.

Voices murmur in the silence,
Echoes of a past embrace.
Fragments linger at the edges,
Fleeting moments, lost in space.

Every heartbeat a reminder,
That stillness holds its breath.
In the curve of shadows dancing,
I find the pulse of death.

Yet in this tender twilight,
Hope rises with the sun.
To dwell within the interstice,
Where worlds continue to run.

The Merging of Two Spheres

Two realms twine like lovers,
Their whispers blend and sigh.
Mysteries weave their fabric,
    As twilight greets the sky.

Between the known and the unseen,
    A threshold softly glows.
In the flutter of heartbeats,
The bridge of longing grows.

Stars shimmer in the darkness,
A dance of fate and chance.
Each step evokes connection,
In the sacred, tender dance.

A tapestry of futures,
Woven with threads of dreams.
In the merging of two spheres,
    Life flows like silver streams.

Portals of the Soul's Journey

Each heart holds a doorway,
To realms we've never known.
In the stillness of the moment,
The seeds of truth are sown.

Whispers brush like feathers,
Across the surface of dreams.
They beckon from the shadows,
Promising hope that gleams.

Through portals etched in silence,
We wander, hand in hand.
With courage as our compass,
We traverse this mystic land.

Every step is revelation,
With lessons carved in light.
The soul's journey ignites us,
As we navigate the night.

Echoes of Duality

In the whispers of the night,
Two souls dance in pure light.
Fleeting moments interlace,
Mirror images find their place.

Reflections from the past,
Each shadow that we cast,
In silence, secrets unfold,
Stories waiting to be told.

With every step, we sway,
In this beautiful ballet.
Two hearts beat as one,
Until the day is done.

In the echoes, we reside,
With our fears set aside.
Embracing what we feel,
In this world, we are real.

Thresholds of Unseen Realms

At the edge of waking dreams,
Where nothing's as it seems,
Veils of mist softly part,
Igniting the wandering heart.

Paths of light and shadow weave,
Infinite webs we believe.
Each step a whispered chance,
Guiding the mystic dance.

Cascades of bright unknown,
In this realm, we are not alone.
Threads of fate intertwine,
Binding yours gently with mine.

Beyond what eyes can see,
Lies the truth of you and me.
With courage, let's explore,
The magic behind the door.

The Space Where Shadows Meet

In the twilight's tender glow,
Shadows stretch and gently flow.
Between the light and dark,
Is where we leave our mark.

A canvas painted with our fears,
Mixed with laughter and with tears.
In the silence, echoes play,
Mapping the paths of yesterday.

Here, whispers share their tales,
Beneath the moon, the night unveils.
Between breath and heartbeat's song,
Is where we truly belong.

When dusk and dawn collide,
In this space, we confide.
Finding solace, we retreat,
In the shadows, we are complete.

Driftwood on a Forgotten Shore

Washed up by the ocean's tide,
Stories of the sea abide.
Each piece tells a tale untold,
Of adventures brave and bold.

Weathered by the winds of time,
In the silence, they still chime.
Fragments of a life once lived,
In their essence, hope is sieved.

Nestled in the grains of sand,
Carried by the sea's command.
Each curve and knot speaks of fate,
Remnants of what we create.

On this shore, so far away,
In stillness, dreams can sway.
Driftwood memories we adore,
Holding on, forevermore.

Starlit Paths of Ambiguity

In shadows where the starlight bends,
Whispers of fate play hide and seek.
Every choice a path that quite depends,
On dreams we chase, yet dare not speak.

Through twilight's veil, the dancers glide,
With laughter lost in cosmic streams.
A tangled web where doubts reside,
Unraveling our secret dreams.

Navigating through the midnight haze,
With every heartbeat, worlds collide.
While echoes fade in endless ways,
We wander forth, our hearts our guide.

In starlit paths, we find our way,
Embracing truth and mystery.
Together here, come what may,
We paint the night with history.

Floating on a Nebula's Edge

Suspended high in violet skies,
We drift through realms of colored light.
Where thoughts are stars, and dreams arise,
In nebulous clouds, we take flight.

With each soft pulse, a story spins,
Galaxies swaying in dance divine.
Our whispers merge, where silence wins,
And time forgets to draw the line.

We wander through this cosmic sea,
Emotions woven in shades of dawn.
Boundless space cradles you and me,
As we float on, till night is gone.

The edge of dreams, we softly tread,
In the quiet hum of the unknown.
Where every breath the universe fed,
Calls us home, to stars, we've grown.

The Convergence of Two Skies

When twilight kisses day goodnight,
Two skies converge in hues of grace.
One whispers love, the other fright,
In their embrace, we find our place.

Stars ignite in a harmonious blend,
Painting tales of fate upon our hearts.
Where every story weaves and bends,
New beginnings rise as old departs.

In fleeting moments, our eyes align,
Reflecting wonders held in each fold.
With quiet courage, two lives entwine,
A tapestry of dreams retold.

In this convergence, time stands still,
Two souls united, no signs of strife.
As dawn breaks softly, hearts will thrill,
To know this blend births a new life.

Interludes of the Uncharted

Across the seas of untraveled dreams,
We sail on currents wild and free.
Charting the depth of our silent schemes,
In a cosmos vast, just you and me.

Every wave whispers secrets untold,
While we dance to the rhythm of fate.
The stories of wonders waiting to unfold,
Captivating in the twilight's gate.

Boundless horizons greet our eyes,
With each interlude, a beckoning call.
Navigating realms beneath the skies,
Together rising, we'll never fall.

In this journey, hand in hand we'll roam,
Discovering magic where shadows blend.
In the uncharted, we've found our home,
With love as the compass, together we'll mend.

A Garden Where Seasons Amalgamate

In the garden blooms a mix,
Where summer's warmth meets autumn's cold.
Petals whisper, secrets fix,
As nature's tales are gently told.

Springtime buds in winter's nap,
Colors brush the canvas bright.
Life awakens from its trap,
Dancing under morning light.

Leaves exchange their vibrant hues,
Fragrant breezes softly sigh.
Each moment, a blend of views,
In harmony as days pass by.

Time weaves tales in every glance,
The seasons join, a waltz divine.
In this space, we glimpse a chance,
As nature's heart begins to shine.

At the Brink of Something New

Beneath the stars, a journey beckons,
Futures bright with untold dreams.
Hope ignites, each moment reckons,
Whispers trace through moonlit beams.

In shadows cast by fading light,
We stand poised at the great divide.
The unknown feels both calm and bright,
A tide of change we cannot hide.

With every breath, the world expands,
Inviting us to take a stride.
With open hearts and willing hands,
We dare to leap, let fears subside.

Together we embrace the dawn,
Where every step uncovers clues.
In the silence, hope is drawn,
At the brink of something new.

Echoes of Dusk and Dawn

As day surrenders to the night,
Whispers hover in twilight's glow.
Stars awaken, sharp and bright,
In dreams where shadowed thoughts can flow.

The sun breathes life with every rise,
Painting skies in gold and red.
In each moment, the world replies,
Carrying echoes of what's said.

Between the hours, silence reigns,
A canvas painted soft and true.
Each whisper holds both joy and pains,
In the dance of night, fresh and new.

Caught between the dusk and dawn,
Life's rhythms pulse, both bold and shy.
Here lies the beauty, never gone,
In every heartbeat, hope will fly.

Shadows of the Unseen Path

In the forest, shadows play,
Concealing pathways of the night.
Whispers linger, thoughts may stray,
Guided only by the light.

Steps echo on the winding trail,
Where mysteries begin to weave.
Through whispered winds, we must not fail,
To chase the dreams that we believe.

Every turn a tale untold,
Every stumble, part of fate.
In the dark, our hearts turn bold,
Trusting where we navigate.

Together in this quiet roam,
We find the strength in shadows cast.
Each step leads us closer home,
On the unseen path, we'll last.

The Silent Pulse of Harmony

In whispers soft, the breeze does sigh,
Each note a promise, soaring high.
The heartbeat of the veil so thin,
Where peace resides, and dreams begin.

Through rustling leaves, the secrets sway,
A symphony of night and day.
Nature's song, a gentle hum,
In every pulse, the world feels numb.

The river flows, a liquid tune,
Reflections dance beneath the moon.
In stillness, beauty finds its way,
A silent pulse that guides the day.

So listen close, let worries cease,
Embrace the quiet, feel the peace.
In harmony, our spirits vie,
For fleeting moments passing by.

Whirling in the In-Between

A dance of shadows, light unfolds,
The world between both young and old.
In twilight's grasp, we spin and sway,
As time suspends, it fades away.

The echoes of what once has been,
A fleeting glimpse of all unseen.
Through swirling mists, we chase a dream,
In every turn, a hidden theme.

The heartbeat quickens, yet we pause,
To find the stillness in our cause.
In moments caught, we lose and find,
A greater truth that binds mankind.

So whirling forth, we embrace the now,
In gratitude, take a humble bow.
For in this dance, we weave our thread,
The tapestry of life, it's said.

The Unfolding of an Unseen Map

In quiet folds of ancient pages,
Lie stories whispered through the ages.
A labyrinth of dreams and fears,
With ink that shimmers through our tears.

Each stroke a guide, a path to trace,
Where hope and doubt entwine their space.
The compass sways, yet finds its way,
Into the light of a brand new day.

From rugged peaks to valleys deep,
The secrets of the heart we keep.
In shadows cast, the truth appears,
An unseen map drawn through the years.

So take a step, let courage lead,
In every choice, plant every seed.
For in this journey, we unfold,
A tale of wonders yet untold.

Beyond the Silhouette of Existence

In shadows deep, we seek the light,
A silhouette beyond our sight.
What lies beyond this fleeting guise,
A truth that glimmers in disguise.

Each moment whispers, softly fades,
In stillness, find the paths we've made.
Beyond the flesh, the spirit soars,
In realms unseen, it gently explores.

With every breath, a world ignites,
In silent space, the heart takes flight.
For life is more than skin and bone,
A vast expanse where we are known.

So let us reach beyond the veil,
Embrace the mystery, let love prevail.
For in this dance of spark and soul,
We find our place, we become whole.

Places Where Time Stumbles

In the quiet of the forest's breath,
Time stumbles over stones and leaves,
Whispers of ages linger soft,
As sunlight dances through the eaves.

In the market's vibrant, thrumming heart,
Moments collide like colors in a swirl,
Each laugh and cry a fleeting part,
Where yesterday and tomorrow unfurl.

By the shores where the waves caress,
Eons wash away in foamy sighs,
Footprints trace tales of happiness,
As the horizon swallows the skies.

In the shadows of the ancient walls,
Time hesitates, then slowly spins,
Echoes of lovers' whispered calls,
Where the tale of life begins and ends.

The Unseen Junction

At the crossroads where dreams converge,
Whispers linger like a gentle breeze,
Paths entwined by fate's urging surge,
A silent compass points with ease.

Beneath the stars that guide the night,
Choices flicker, a dance of fate,
Each path a promise, soft and bright,
The unseen holds what hearts create.

With every step, a new refrain,
The echoes of a choice once made,
At this junction, joy and pain,
Two roads entwined in twilight's shade.

In the stillness, brave or meek,
The heart chooses its honest song,
In this junction, all must speak,
What feels the right will never be wrong.

Dreams Drenched in Dusk

In the hour where shadows blend,
Dreams unfold like petals wide,
Painted skies begin to mend,
As daylight softly chooses to hide.

Through the whispers of the cool night air,
Visions dance on the edge of sight,
Each breath a secret, fragile and rare,
Cradled in the arms of twilight's light.

With stars that blink in endless flow,
Thoughts sail softly on the breeze,
Drenched in hues of evening's glow,
Where quiet moments aim to please.

As time stands still and heartbeats swell,
Dreams arise from dusk's embrace,
In the silence, stories tell,
Of whispering hopes in a sacred space.

Passages of the Heart's Whisper

In corridors where silence reigns,
The heart's whispers softly tread,
Through beats that rise and fall like rains,
Paths of emotion, rarely said.

Glimmers of hope in twilight's grace,
Each pulse a story waiting to bloom,
Passages etched in time and space,
Where shadows dance inside the room.

With every sigh, a secret shared,
The tender truths that break the night,
In these passages, love is bared,
Eclipsing fear with gentle light.

In dreams where whispers intertwine,
The heart finds courage in each plea,
Through hidden paths, a love divine,
In every word, the soul runs free.

Liminal Landscapes

Between dusk and dawn we tread,
Where shadows dance and whispers spread.
The air is thick with dreams untold,
In spaces where the brave unfold.

Paths of twilight beckon near,
A journey blurred, both strange and clear.
The edges melt like colors blend,
In fleeting moments, we ascend.

Echoes linger in the air,
A silent call, a waking dare.
Where boundaries blur, we become free,
In liminal lands, just you and me.

With each step, the world resets,
In these landscapes, no regrets.
We wander forth, the heart's command,
In twilight realms, we understand.

A Canvas of Unfinished Stories

Brushstrokes linger, tales unwritten,
On canvas soft, where dreams are smitten.
Colors clash and softly blend,
In every hue, new worlds extend.

Characters dance in vibrant light,
Whispers of fate, in day and night.
Each line reveals a life once bold,
A story waiting to unfold.

Fragments of time in palettes bright,
Echoing laughter, love, and fright.
A canvas full of hope and fear,
Unfinished tales that draw us near.

With every stroke, the past remains,
A tapestry of joys and pains.
In every corner, a mystery glows,
A canvas rich with all that flows.

The Quietude of Merging Stories

In whispered tones, our tales collide,
The quietude where hearts reside.
Interwoven paths, like threads of silk,
In stillness, we share our dreams and ilk.

Moments converge in gentle ease,
Life's stories blend like leaves in breeze.
Each narrative a subtle song,
In unity, where we belong.

Behind closed eyes, the visions blend,
In silent chapters, we transcend.
The quietude holds truths so deep,
In the fusion of dreams we keep.

Together, we navigate the night,
Embracing shadows, seeking light.
With every breath, our worlds align,
In merging stories, stars will shine.

Ripples in Mixed Waters

When currents mingle, secrets sway,
Ripples dance in the light of day.
Reflections shimmer, stories flow,
In mixed waters, truths we know.

Each drop a tale, each wave a thought,
In chaos, calmness can be sought.
The waters warm, then turn to chill,
In shifting tides, there lies a thrill.

Echoes ripple through the stream,
Awakening forgotten dreams.
In depths concealed, the treasures wait,
To guide us through our fate's own gate.

Together, we become the part,
Of swirling waters, art to heart.
In every ripple, life reveals,
The beauty found in how it heals.

The Sighs of Forgotten Places

In corners dark, whispers remain,
Echoes of laughter, layers of pain.
Dust dances lightly on aged walls,
Stories linger where silence calls.

Beneath the roots of a weathered tree,
Memories murmur, lost but free.
Time weaves shadows, soft in embrace,
In the sighs of these forgotten places.

The breeze carries secrets, soft as the night,
Footsteps of wanderers long out of sight.
With every sigh, a tale reclaims,
In the heart of the past, the echo remains.

Each stone holds a dream that once was bright,
Beneath the veil of the falling light.
In every crevice, a hope yet glows,
In these spaces where no one goes.

The Overlap of Possibilities

In a world spun with threads of fate,
Paths intertwine, both early and late.
Choices like feathers in the breeze,
Drifting softly among the trees.

Moments collide like stars in the sky,
Infinite dreams that dare to fly.
Each heartbeat a chance, a spark to ignite,
In the overlap of shadows and light.

Whispers of what could be softly tread,
On the edge of the dreams we've left unsaid.
Threads of tomorrow crossed with today,
In this tapestry where hopes play.

The echo of laughter, a glimpse of a tear,
A dance of decisions, both far and near.
Every pathway a story yet told,
In the overlap where futures unfold.

Enigmatic Pathways

Winding trails through the forest deep,
Secrets hidden where shadows creep.
Each step taken, a puzzle unfolds,
Mysteries whispered by ancient folds.

Under the gaze of a waning moon,
Nature's silence hums a haunting tune.
Pathways shimmer with stories begun,
Drenched in silver from the setting sun.

Footprints trace the lines of the wise,
Guided by starlight that never lies.
Curves and turns lead to the unknown,
In these enigmatic pathways, we're never alone.

Every rustle, a hint of the past,
In the garden of riddles, we're spellbound and cast.
With each heartbeat, the journey goes on,
On these winding roads where dreams are drawn.

The Twilight Realm Unfolds

In the hush where day meets night,
A dance of hues, a fading light.
Crickets sing in the soft, cool air,
As shadows stretch in the dusk's sweet glare.

The horizon blushes, wrapped in gold,
Whispers of secrets long ago told.
Silhouettes linger on the edge of sight,
In the twilight realm where dreams take flight.

Misty shapes drift through the trees,
Carrying tales on a gentle breeze.
Stars awaken in the velvet sky,
As the twilight beckons with a soft sigh.

In this moment, all things are one,
The day is ending, the night begun.
A realm of wonder, where magic unfolds,
In the twilight, each story molds.

Lingering at the Crossroads

At dusk where paths collide,
Shadows lengthen, dreams reside.
Choices whisper through the trees,
Caught between the sighing leaves.

Footsteps echo on the stone,
A journey forged yet to be known.
Voices linger, soft and clear,
Guiding hearts with hope and fear.

The signs invite with gentle grace,
Beneath the moon, this sacred place.
While stars align, the night unfolds,
The future waits, a tale untold.

In silence, possibilities bloom,
A symphony of hope and gloom.
Lingering here, a breath in time,
Life's many paths, a dance in rhyme.

The Horizon's Breath

Beyond the veil where daylight fades,
The horizon breathes, a golden cascade.
Colors blend in a cosmic play,
Whispers of night greet the day.

Waves crash softly, a rhythmic dance,
In the twilight, dreams take their chance.
The sun bows low, a fleeting kiss,
Moments linger in twilight's bliss.

Clouds drift slowly, stories they tell,
Of timeless journeys, where spirits dwell.
Each hue of dusk, a brushstroke bold,
Carving memories from the gold.

In the silence, a promise stirs,
A gentle hope, like a heart that purrs.
The horizon waits, forever in sight,
Breathing dreams into the night.

Spectres of the Crossing

In shadows deep, the lost convene,
Spectres hover, silent and keen.
Echoes of paths that fade away,
Whisper secrets of yesterday.

A sigh of winds, a fleeting glance,
Ghostly figures in a trance.
Veils of night, they drift and weave,
Carrying tales that none believe.

Each crossroad marked by what's been lost,
Memories linger, paying the cost.
They beckon softly, hands outstretched,
Binding their stories, tightly etched.

In twilight's grasp, they softly tread,
Carrying burdens, dreams unsaid.
Spectres wander, endlessly freed,
In the silence, we plant the seed.

Flickers of an Unwritten Tale

In the quiet night where dreams ignite,
Flickers of whispers take to flight.
Pages blank, a story untold,
The spark of imagination bold.

Words unspoken dance in the air,
Ideas swirl with a vibrant flare.
Hope weaves magic in every sigh,
A tapestry of thoughts that fly.

Ink-stains mark the heart's canvas wide,
Where every choice is a shifting tide.
Moments captured in fleeting light,
An unwritten tale, hidden from sight.

In the stillness, we find our voice,
Amidst the chaos, we make our choice.
Flickers of life, bright and frail,
Shape the echoes of the unwritten tale.

Hazy Journeys at the Crossroads

At twilight's hush, the paths converge,
Whispers of fate, in silence urge.
Fog drapes gently on all we seek,
Questions linger, the answers bleak.

Footsteps falter on shifting sand,
Dreams collide, slip through our hand.
Choices loom, both faint and bright,
Navigating through the fading light.

The heart's compass spins around,
Lost in a maze, where hope is found.
In every turn, a story we weave,
In hazy journeys, we dare believe.

Crossroads beckon, a chance to choose,
We step forward and learn to lose.
Yet through the haze, the path will clear,
With every heartbeat, we persevere.

The Dimensional Drift

In realms unseen, we float and glide,
Through layers of time, we slip and slide.
Dimensions merge, then break apart,
The universe dances, a cosmic art.

Stars collide in a vibrant embrace,
Each moment shifts, a new face in space.
Gravity bends, a dreamlike flow,
In this drift, we learn to go slow.

Voices echo in a void so deep,
Whispers of wisdom, ancient and steep.
Every pulse of light, a chance we take,
In the dimensional drift, we awake.

As shadows stretch and colors blend,
In every journey, we find a friend.
With courage to leap through the unknown,
In this drift, we are never alone.

Gossamer Threads of Existence

Delicate strands, woven with care,
Each tiny moment dances in air.
Life's tapestry, both fragile and grand,
Intertwined souls, hand in hand.

Every breath, a whisper of light,
Gossamer dreams take their flight.
Fragile but fierce, these threads we spin,
Weaving stories of loss and win.

Connections sparkle in twilight's glow,
Each heartbeat reflects what we know.
In the web of life, both near and far,
We find our place, like a guiding star.

Time ebbs softly, a river's flow,
Through gossamer threads, love will grow.
For every thread that frays or bends,
A new beginning, as hope ascends.

The Edge of Reality

In shadows cast where dreams collide,
We traverse the edge, where doubts reside.
Reality shifts like grains of sand,
At the brink, we take a stand.

Mirrors shatter, reflections change,
What was once certain, feels so strange.
Fingers brush the unseen veil,
At the edge of reality, we sail.

Silent screams echo in the night,
Caught in a dance between wrong and right.
With every heartbeat, a glimpse anew,
At the edge, we dare to pursue.

Questions rise on wings of thought,
In the twilight, reality's caught.
Embrace the blur, let go the fight,
For at the edge, we find the light.

The Silent Symphony of Overlap

In shadows where we softly meet,
A whisper lingers, bittersweet.
Unseen notes in twilight's grace,
Harmonies found in an empty space.

Threads of silence weave our song,
In quiet places, where we belong.
Each heartbeat's echo, a tender sign,
Binding your rhythm gently with mine.

Moments intertwine, a beautiful blur,
In the stillness, our spirits stir.
A symphony of sighs takes flight,
In the hush, we find our light.

Fleeting echoes, a timeless thread,
In silence, words remain unsaid.
Together, as one, we gently sway,
In the silent night, we lose our way.

Threads of Two Existence

Two souls dancing on the edge,
Each promise made, a quiet pledge.
In the tapestry, colors blend,
With every thread, a story penned.

Woven paths that cross and part,
Every heartbeat, a work of art.
Through every joy and every tear,
In the silence, we still draw near.

Glimmers of hope in woven strands,
An intricate map of gentle hands.
Together we stand, yet diverge,
In the loom of life, our spirits surge.

Threads of fate bind us tight,
In the dark, we'll find our light.
With every twist, a dance of grace,
In this journey, we find our place.

A Dance of Fleeting Moments

Time slips softly through our hands,
Like grains of sand on distant shores.
In every glance, a story stands,
A dance of moments, forever yours.

We waltz beneath the starlit sky,
With laughter echoing in the dark.
In every breath, a soft goodbye,
Yet in each beat, we leave a mark.

Fleeting whispers in the night air,
Captured in the shadows' embrace.
A dance of dreams, lights flicker where
Time pauses, just to hold our grace.

Moments blend like colors bright,
In this tapestry, we entwine.
A dance of hearts, a shared delight,
Together, love's sweet design.

Twilight's Embrace

As daylight fades, the stars appear,
In twilight's glow, we find our peace.
With gentle whispers, night draws near,
In darkness, all our worries cease.

A canvas stretched 'neath twilight skies,
Colors bleeding, merging slow.
In this hush where silence lies,
The heart's true rhythm starts to flow.

Hand in hand, beneath the moon,
We dance to melodies unheard.
In every shadow, a sweet tune,
With every breath, a promise stirred.

Twilight wraps its arms so tight,
Holding moments, serene and bright.
In the stillness, love's embrace,
In twilight's arms, we find our place.

Gazing through Fractured Lenses

In the twilight's fading glow,
Shadows dance on walls below.
Thoughts collide in shattered glass,
Memories fade, yet moments last.

Every glance a fleeting dream,
Reality bends at the seam.
Fragments tell a story new,
Colors blend in shades askew.

Through the cracks, the light will seep,
Whispers from the depths will creep.
The heart beats in silent cries,
Longing whispered through the skies.

In the chaos, clarity's found,
In the lost, the hope is bound.
Gazing through the fractured piece,
Finding solace, finding peace.

The Unfolding of Silver Pathways

Beneath the stars, the journey starts,
Silver threads weave countless parts.
Paths unseen begin to glow,
In the night where dreams will flow.

Each step taken, whispers rise,
Guiding hearts where truth lies.
Softly spoken, tales unfold,
In the shimmer, secrets told.

While the moonlight bathes the earth,
Every shadow hints of birth.
Through the dark, the spark will shine,
In the spaces, fate aligns.

With each choice, a story spins,
Following where the light begins.
Onward through the silver gleam,
Life emerges from the dream.

Silent Conversations of Distant Echoes

Whispers linger in the air,
Voices call from everywhere.
Echoes dance with tones so sweet,
In the silence, thoughts compete.

Memories woven, heartstrings tugged,
In the stillness, dreams are snugged.
Every sound a note from past,
Moments cherished, fading fast.

Conversations lost in time,
Eternal rhythms, soft and grime.
Bursting forth in muted cries,
Underneath the endless skies.

In the void, the soul will soar,
Finding peace on distant shores.
Silent echoes reflect what's true,
In each heartbeat, I find you.

The Dual Nature of Being

In every heartbeat, shadows play,
Light and dark in a delicate sway.
Life's canvas, struck with hues,
Every choice a path to choose.

The sun rises, the moon will fall,
Beauty blooms, while shadows call.
Joy and sorrow, intertwined,
In the chaos, peace we find.

Every laugh, a hint of pain,
In the joy, there's room for rain.
A dance of contrasts, bold and deep,
In the wake of dreams, we leap.

Embrace the dance of light and shade,
In the balance, life is made.
Finding grace in every strife,
In the duality, we find life.

Murmurs from the Threshold

Soft whispers breathe through night,
Hushed tones that dance with light.
Shadows flicker on the wall,
Echoes rise, invite their call.

A restless heart, a cautious sigh,
Waiting for the stars to fly.
Dreams that linger, hold their ground,
In this hush, the world resounds.

Voices trapped in twilight's grip,
Fearless souls begin to slip.
In the silence, hope is found,
Murmurs weave a wondrous sound.

Step by step, the door ajar,
Leading where the wonders are.
With each breath, we take our place,
In this realm of soft embrace.

Navigating the Nebulous

In a realm of haze and mist,
Lost thoughts and dreams twist and twist.
Stars concealed, yet still they glow,
Guiding paths through veils of woe.

Amidst the chaos, calm resides,
Waves of doubt, the heart abides.
Fragments of light, they pierce the dark,
Fleeting hopes leave their mark.

Journey forth through shadows deep,
Where silence holds the secrets steep.
Each step taken, a breath anew,
In this dance with the unknown too.

With the pulse of the universe near,
Navigating what we hold dear.
Through the fog, we seek the bright,
Trusting the heart, embracing the light.

Footprints in the Void

In the emptiness, we tread,
Marking paths where few have led.
Each impression tells a tale,
Of courage found in every veil.

Silent echoes fill the air,
Remnants of a distant prayer.
What was lost now seeks to find,
Footprints left by the divine.

In the dark, we trace the lines,
Connecting dots through cosmic signs.
Through the void, our spirits soar,
Each footprint whispers, 'Explore more.'

A canvas blank, yet rich with dreams,
We weave our journey through the seams.
With every step, new worlds unfold,
In the vastness, stories told.

Reflections on the Misty Border

Where the land meets the horizon,
Shadows linger, softly rising.
A border drawn in misty hues,
Secrets held beneath the blues.

Each glance reflects a fleeting thought,
In this space, the world is caught.
Mirrors of the heart collide,
In the stillness, dreams abide.

Gentle waves lap at the shore,
Whispers tell of tales of yore.
With each ripple, memories blend,
At the border, where dreams transcend.

In the twilight, echoes gleam,
Those reflections, a silent dream.
As we stand on this divide,
In the mist, our souls confide.

Whispers in the Veil

In the hush of night, secrets gleam,
Muffled voices dance, lost in a dream.
Shadows twirl softly in moonlit grace,
A quiet symphony, time's gentle embrace.

Fingers trace edges of what once was,
Breath of the past lingers, a soft pause.
Veils of remembrance drape like a shroud,
Whispers of stories, both tender and loud.

Echoes of laughter float on the breeze,
Sprinklings of magic, heart's uncharted keys.
Through the fabric of night, wishes take flight,
Cradled in dreams, enshrouded in light.

Threads of existence weave in the dark,
In the tapestry's heart lies the spark.
Each whisper a promise, each sigh a song,
In the veil of the night, we all belong.

Tides of the In-Between

The ocean breathes soft with ebbing tides,
Secrets well up where the darkness hides.
Moments suspended, neither here nor there,
Drifting like whispers in salt-kissed air.

Footprints erased by the waves' embrace,
Echoes of laughter fade without a trace.
In the currents of time, we search for the line,
Between what is sacred and what is divine.

Carried by dreams on a sea of gray,
Navigating paths where shadows play.
Each heart holds a compass, guiding us through,
The space in between, where wishes renew.

Sails of the spirit, unfurl and soar,
Embracing the journey, forever explore.
In tides of the in-between, we find our way,
A dance of existence, come what may.

Crossing the Rubicon of Dreams

Steps echo softly on ancient ground,
Crossroads loom where fate is found.
A river of choice flows deep and wide,
Courage ignites as fears collide.

Beyond the horizon, the sun may rise,
Unraveling truths behind gentle lies.
Each heartbeat whispers, venture ahead,
Across the divide, where dreams are bred.

Like embers glowing in the still of the night,
Visions take form, becoming our light.
With each breath drawn, the world expands,
We forge our paths with hopeful hands.

Crossing the Rubicon, the moment is now,
No turning back, we take the vow.
In the fabric of dreams, our stories entwine,
A tapestry woven, forever divine.

Fragments of Twilight

As the sun dips low, a canvas unfolds,
Brush strokes of crimson, lavender, gold.
Whispers of twilight, soft-spoken and brief,
A fleeting farewell, a moment of grief.

Stars peek through curtains of silken night,
Glimmers of hope in the fading light.
Night gathers 'round like a comforting cloak,
Ancient tales shared in the hush, softly spoke.

Fragments of time shimmer and sway,
In the stillness, remnants of day.
Moonlight spills secrets on slumbering dreams,
Stitching together life's delicate seams.

In twilight's embrace, our hearts intertwine,
A dance of existence, forever divine.
Each fragment a story, a flicker, a spark,
In the twilight's grip, we leave our mark.

Dances in the Gray

In twilight's soft embrace they sway,
Shadows blend and colors play.
Laughter whispers through the mist,
As daylight fades, they coexist.

Footsteps echo in the night,
A silent waltz, a fleeting flight.
Underneath the silver skies,
Dreams awaken, hopes arise.

With grace they twirl, in silence bound,
In the beauty of what's found.
Between the dark and gleaming light,
They dance beneath the stars so bright.

Together they embrace the hue,
In every shade, a love so true.
For in the gray, they find their song,
In every moment, they belong.

Between Silence and Sound

Whispers float on a gentle breeze,
In the stillness, hearts find ease.
Between the beats where echoes lie,
True feelings surface, shy yet spry.

A symphony of hidden thought,
In every pause, connection sought.
The hush of night, a canvas bare,
In silence lies an answered prayer.

Notes entwined in warm embrace,
An ever-changing, sacred space.
Between the silence and the roar,
We find the meaning we explore.

With every heartbeat, whispers grow,
Unseen currents gently flow.
In the balance of what's profound,
We learn to dance, both lost and found.

The Echo Chamber of Possibilities

In corridors where dreams take flight,
Reflections shimmer, bold and bright.
Each thought a ripple, a chance to chase,
In this chamber, we find our place.

Voices murmur, futures weave,
In every choice, a chance to believe.
Resonating through time and space,
In echoes, we discover grace.

Paths entwined, like vines that climb,
In whispers soft, we trace the rhyme.
Possibilities shimmer, dance and sway,
They guide our feet along the way.

In this circle of endless dreams,
We strum the heartstrings, hear the beams.
Within each echo, life unfolds,
As stories rich with hope are told.

Threads of Two Realms

Woven tightly, hearts in tune,
A tapestry by light of moon.
In the fabric where dreams abide,
Two realms entwined, love as the guide.

One realm of shadows, one of light,
In the balance, both ignite.
Stitched together, they create,
A journey filled with hope and fate.

With every thread, a tale is spun,
In every color, a life begun.
Through ups and downs, they find their way,
In this dance, they choose to stay.

Together they forge the path ahead,
In whispers soft, their dreams are fed.
Threads of two realms, so deftly sewn,
In love's embrace, they're never alone.

The Liminal Dance of Time

In shadows where the daylight fades,
We tread the line of dusk and dawn.
Whispers echo in the twilight glades,
  Moments linger, then are gone.

Each heartbeat marks the passing hour,
  A flicker caught in fleeting grace.
Time dances lightly, swift as flower,
  Petals drifting from their place.

In breath between the now and then,
We sway, suspended, lost in dreams.
Beneath the weave of joy and pain,
We glide along forgotten streams.

So let us twirl in soft embrace,
As time unravels, thread by thread.
  In this liminal, sacred space,
Our spirits dance, and fears are shed.

Secrets of the In-Between

Between the worlds of dark and light,
Lies a space where secrets dwell.
In hushed tones, whispers take flight,
Stories no one dares to tell.

The bridge where silence meets the sound,
Holds treasures hidden from the eye.
In shadows deep, the truth is found,
Beneath the veil, the reasons lie.

Time bends within this fragile frame,
Where echoes of the past reside.
Each moment carries a new name,
Chasing dreams from side to side.

Unlock the door, release the key,
To realms where all is yet to be.
Embrace the magic of the scene,
And dance within the in-between.

Crossing the Fractured Line

A chasm deep, a fractured line,
Where dreams collide and hopes may fray.
We gather courage, hearts align,
To step beyond the light of day.

With trembling hands, we reach for foe,
The shadows twist in pale moonlight.
In unison, we face the woe,
Transcending boundaries, claim our right.

Each whispered doubt, a fleeting guest,
Yet in the chaos, strength is found.
We rise together, souls blessed,
To mend the line that once was bound.

So cross with me, uncharted space,
Where courage blooms in fierce embrace.
In every fracture, hope will shine,
Through every step, the stars align.

Floating on the Edge of Being

Adrift upon a sea of thought,
We navigate the waves of time.
In quiet longing, wisdom sought,
A dance of rhythms, soft and sublime.

The edge of being, tattered seam,
Where thoughts and dreams begin to blend.
In fragile balance, we dare to dream,
With every breath, we seek to mend.

Suspended in this liminal flight,
We find our peace amidst the roar.
In whispered voices, we ignite,
A spark of life forevermore.

So let us float, entwined and free,
Along the currents, wild and wide.
Embracing all that we can be,
In every heartbeat, love our guide.

Memories of a Distant Echo

In the twilight of fading light,
Whispers of yesteryears play.
Softly drifting, time takes flight,
Lost in shadows of yesterday.

Footsteps echo on the ground,
Carried by the wind's caress.
In silence, lost memories found,
In moments that we can't possess.

Images dance in dreams so wild,
Fragments of what used to be.
Each face a long-forgotten child,
A mirror of the heart's decree.

Yet in the distance, love remains,
A melody in soft refrain.
Through laughter and through all the pains,
The echo calls us home again.

Threads of the Invisible

Woven in the fabric of night,
Whispers bind the soul so tight.
Elusive hands that intertwine,
A tapestry of fate divine.

Colors shift in the unseen loom,
Weaving dreams in silent gloom.
Each thread a path we cannot trace,
Binding time in tender grace.

Through every step, a choice we weave,
Invisible, yet bold, we cleave.
In shadows, light begins to show,
The dance of life, a subtle flow.

And as the dawn begins to break,
The threads of gold we choose to make.
In unity, our hearts awake,
While paths of love begin to stake.

The Crossroads of Being

In the stillness where dreams collide,
Two roads stretch, each a guide.
Choices linger in the air,
Whispers of fate, a sacred dare.

One road shines with golden light,
The other cloaked in shadowed night.
Each step taken feels so real,
At this brink, what fate does reveal?

Voices call from both the ways,
Promises of bright and dark days.
A heart divided, torn in two,
Which path, dear soul, do you pursue?

Amidst the wonder and the fear,
A truth unfolds, so crystal clear.
For every choice, a chance to grow,
In every heart, the seeds we sow.

Veils That Separate the Known

In twilight's grasp where shadows blend,
Veils rise softly, meanings bend.
The known retreats to secret lands,
As time slips softly through our hands.

Mysteries wrapped in tales untold,
Flicker like stars, bright and bold.
Between the lines, truths are found,
Hidden echoes, a sacred sound.

With every breath, we seek to touch,
What lies beyond, we yearn so much.
Yet in the veils, the silence sings,
Revealing all that wonder brings.

So let us wander through the dim,
Embracing all that feels like whim.
For in the haze, the heart can see,
The beauty of the mystery.

The Unraveled Tapestry of Existence

Threads of life weave in and out,
Colors blend amidst the shout.
Patterns formed in joy, in pain,
In this dance, we break the chain.

Stories whispered through the years,
In the silence, echo fears.
Hope and sorrow wrapped as one,
Underneath the fading sun.

Each moment stitched, a fragile art,
Connecting souls, never apart.
Yet, some threads begin to fray,
Unravels softly, day by day.

In the weave, a lesson lies,
Strength found where the spirit tries.
Through the chaos, beauty grows,
A rich tapestry, life bestows.

Dancing with the Ethereal

In twilight's glow, we take our flight,
With whispered dreams, we chase the night.
Stars alight in cosmic ballet,
We spin and sway, come what may.

Soft shadows meld with silver beams,
In this realm, we dance our dreams.
Echoes linger in the air,
A waltz with spirits, light as air.

Each step leads to the great unknown,
In harmony, we find our home.
The universe sings a timeless song,
As we harmonize, we belong.

Together swaying, hearts collide,
In the ethereal, we confide.
With every twirl, the moment's bliss,
In this dance, we find our kiss.

A Realm on the Brink

Where shadows stretch and silence lingers,
Potentials wait with bated fingers.
The air is thick with untold sights,
Where dreams collide with fleeting lights.

Whispers call from depths unseen,
A precarious edge, where minds convene.
Beneath the surface, mysteries hum,
In every heartbeat, a world becomes.

Fates entwine in the woven mist,
Each choice a path that twists and twists.
An echo of what could have been,
In this realm, we tread between.

Between the now and what lies next,
In balance, our spirits flexed.
The brink invites both fear and grace,
In each heartbeat, we find our place.

The Hidden Corridors of Being

In the quiet, secrets dwell,
Hidden paths, a silent spell.
Each corner turned, a truth revealed,
In the shadows, hearts are healed.

Doorways leading to the soul,
Unraveling tales, we become whole.
In narrow halls of thought and time,
We search for meaning, steeped in rhyme.

Threads of memory intertwine,
In this labyrinth, we define.
With every step, wisdom grows,
In hidden corridors, life flows.

The essence of what's lost, retained,
Through labyrinth's twists, we are sustained.
With open hearts, we seek and find,
The hidden paths of the mind.

Fragments of the Overlap

In shadows where we softly tread,
Whispers echo what is unsaid.
Time dances in the fleeting light,
Weaving threads of day and night.

Each moment holds a hidden gem,
Lost amid the now and then.
Fragments spark in twilight's glow,
Stories linger, ebb and flow.

In silence, secrets intertwine,
Fate's design in fate's own line.
What was past is still in reach,
Lessons learned, yet still to teach.

Through the veil, we chase the dream,
A fleeting glimpse, a shimmering beam.
In this overlap, we find our peace,
A tapestry that will not cease.

The Uncharted Space

Beyond the stars, where wonders sleep,
In uncharted space, our visions leap.
Galaxies whisper tales of old,
In cosmic winds, their stories unfold.

Nebulas swirl in vibrant hues,
Mysteries wrapped in midnight blues.
Each heartbeat sings a distant call,
In this expanse, we rise and fall.

With every step, new worlds arise,
Chasing shadows beneath vast skies.
The universe, a boundless page,
Invites us forth to engage.

Here in the void, we find our spark,
Glimmers of light in the eternal dark.
A journey vast, both strange and bright,
In the uncharted space of night.

Prisms of the Unknown

Through prisms clear, the light cascades,
Refracting dreams in soft parades.
Colors dance in a silent song,
In realms where all the lost belong.

Unlocking doors to hidden hearts,
With gentle hands, the mystery starts.
Each shade tells tales of love and woe,
In the depths of the unknown flow.

Eclipsed by doubt, yet hope persists,
In a haze of existence, we exist.
Navigating paths of fragile grace,
Finding solace in the still space.

Let light reflect on what we fear,
In the unknown, we draw near.
Through every spectrum, we shall roam,
Finding fragments of our home.

Harmonies of Twilight

As twilight falls, the world awakes,
In softest hues, the silence breaks.
The sky, a canvas brushed in gold,
    Tells secrets of the day untold.

Melodies linger in the dusk,
In whispers sweet, a gentle musk.
Night sings softly, a lullaby,
As stars emerge in the velvet sky.

In this hour, the heart takes flight,
Chasing dreams that feel so right.
Harmonies blend in the fading light,
Filling the void with pure delight.

So let us dance in twilight's grace,
Embracing shadows in this space.
Together we'll find what hearts will share,
    In harmonies of twilight, rare.

Whispers Across the Threshold

Soft murmurs drift in twilight air,
Echoes of souls, secrets they share.
Beneath the arch of stars that gleam,
Dreamers wander, lost in a dream.

Footsteps muffled on a dusty path,
Hopes entangled in shadows' wrath.
Crossing lines that fate has drawn,
Finding solace with each dawn.

Voices fade yet linger long,
In the night's embrace, they belong.
A canvas painted with whispered sighs,
Illuminated by midnight skies.

Through the door where silence reigns,
Tales of love and longing, remains.
In echoes soft, we find our way,
Whispers guiding night to day.

The Haze of Uncharted Dreams

In the haze where visions play,
Uncharted paths weave night and day.
Silent hopes on wings of thought,
In every heart, a battle fought.

Colors swirl in the mind's embrace,
Chasing shadows, a fleeting chase.
Grains of time slip through our grasp,
While dreams whisper, and memories clasp.

Each layer hides a silent truth,
A tapestry of forgotten youth.
Navigating through the misty seams,
We wander deep in uncharted dreams.

With every breath, the world expands,
Infinite wonders within our hands.
As dawn breaks, the skies will scream,
Revelations born from fading dreams.

Veil of Twilight Realities

In twilight's hush, where worlds entwine,
Secrets linger, softly divine.
Shadows dance in a gentle breeze,
Holding truths like whispered keys.

Beneath a shroud of starry night,
Dreams emerge, taking flight.
Reality fades, a fleeting sight,
Veil falls softly, lost in light.

Each moment stitched in fragile thread,
Silent stories of the unsaid.
With every heartbeat, fate reveals,
A tapestry of love that heals.

Through the veil where hopes reside,
We find the place where hearts abide.
In twilight's glow, our spirits soar,
Embracing wonders, forevermore.

Where Skies Meet the Unknown

At the edge of earth where skies collide,
Wonders beckon, truth can't hide.
Horizons stretch, inviting the brave,
Whispers of fate in the ocean's wave.

Clouds of mystery, drifting slow,
Every heartbeat ignites a glow.
In the shimmer of stars, adventures wait,
Paths untraveled, we create our fate.

Beneath the arch of endless blue,
The call of dreams pulls us through.
In every glance, a spark ignites,
Where the unknown meets starlit nights.

Together we stand, hand in hand,
Exploring realms, a mystical land.
Where the wild winds softly moan,
We carve our names where skies meet the unknown.